One for the road:

Poems with Pictures

Emily Nash

'THE SEA GIANT'

She stood on a hill one day
and watched the sun arising.
She ran from that summit high
fast, like she was gliding,

to the beach down below,
stretched out and all a glimmer.
The tide was out the beach prepared
with water streaks a glimmer.

Left, the beach it swept along
flat beneath the cliff
which towered still proclaiming
the changing shores that sift.

So gently lapped the waves
upon the giant's edge
so tenderly upon her toes
as if her it did acknowledge.

Indeed each wave was like a sigh
from something old and wise,
who'd seen the sins of all mankind
and watched them die like flies.

And through it all from age to age,
lived on in same routine,
feeding fish and whale and ray
while keeping sands all clean.

Lead by the moon to advance
upon the clay cliff rock,
it takes what it can each time
to feed the deep sea flock.

Today there's a little girl,
the sun says harm her not.
But perhaps on a windy day
she would not keep her spot,

for fear of the crashing waves
and blinding, foaming froth,
that spits from angry gnashing jaws
when the giant is of wroth.

How silky smooth the waters though
when calm his mood it be.
Oh dive and splash
through colours pure!
Ask that life to set you free!

Today the little girl, she runs
a full hour spent in water;
The quiet beast sees her go,
attentive to this daughter.

Having kept all deep sea teeth
and predatory grimace
far below and far away,
that she be safe from menace!

'THE DOGS AND THE GUINEA PIGS'

My sister has long silky hair
she likes to dress it up
in skirts and shiny jewellery
and high heels that go brup brup.

She totters into parties
and charms the boys I've heard
fluttering her eyelids
so they say 'hey, who's that bird?'

But then ofcourse there was the time
when her heart it was taken
by little Fred and Charlie
the guinea pigs forsaken.

I say forsaken as alas
they didn't last for long
when one fine day our dogs
hatched a plan with barking song.

'Get them' yelped the one
jumping on the cage.
'I'm ready' cried the other
as it finally gave way.

My sister did behold it
but alas it was too late;
My brother found the petty bits
on grass and by the gate.

We indulged in a grave funeral
with mournful procession
and buried what was left of them
with tearful intercession.

Litte did we know of course
that justice would be done;
For, between our guinea ghosts
plotting had begun.

The dog who took the lead
would shortly lose her life
as great karma took control,
a twist of traffic strife.

The spirit of one guinea
one morning came upon
the driver of a van
likely going to London.

Through someone else
the other guinea
opened our back gate
to set free the foul-handed dog
that she might meet her fate.

Running down the road
crying 'freedom yee-haaa'
little did she know
at the junction was the car.

As she bounded out with joy
Charlie drove the van
straight over the silly dog
revenge so sweet the plan!

The heavy set van driver
let out a high pitched squeak
and Charlie's spirit leapt forth
from the man of whom we speak.

Poor doggy lying on the road
was dead as a doormat
but her ghost jumped up from her
in leaping, dancing format.

Now we're hoping there's a place
where they are reconciled
dancing altogether now
at peace and undefiled.

'GEEKY INDECISION'

Once there was a silly boy
Who knew not what to do.
Poor soul, he lost his
dad when young
he never had a clue.

At school he took to many things
french and history
physics, music, ancient greek
art even p.e.

His friends called
him a little swot
He had big teeth and glasses.
And success seemed so sure
with each year of
stunning passes.

'02 he went to Manchester
To study at the law.
And though for most it would do
did not quite fit the score.

So he snorted and stuck
out his teeth.
'Why Ma,' one day he said.
'This law business,
really you know
it will drive me nearly dead.'

'I'd better try something else
I see my life in space.
And so to Kings he duly went
and in Aeronautics took his place.

Alas though he was brilliant
and quite excelled them all
'Why dearest ma' one day he said
'I find it all a bore.'

'All this talk of speed of light
and bangs and liquid fuel.
It makes me rather sick you know
I'm in need of a renewal.'

'To focus all one's faculties
on getting way out there
when there is much can be done
on earth that needs repair.'

'There really calls for
minds like mine
for the saving of our planet.
You know dear Ma, environment
that's the boy for me, I've got it!'

'Ha-ha' he snorts and
packs his bags
'to Nottingham I'll go.
Environmental science
into that myself I'll throw.'

Alas a year gone by and see him
shake from side to side his head
'Why Ma', 'WHAT NOW'
she screams all tense
'But you haven't heard
what I've said.'

'I was not blessed with
brains like mine
to look all day at dirt.
Soil is all very well
for standing on I'd assert.

'But surely even
worms themselves
have more a break than I
from digestion of such
boring stuff.
This course is meant to try!'

'And so my dear' he lifts his hand
and points a lanky finger.
On this I have decided
to turn to the life-bringer.

'Why focus on material things
when there is God in heaven.
To what greater heights
could I aspire
than the study of the brethren?'

And so he puts his glasses on
and clicks his gangly neck.
'To bible college mother dear,
my life is now in check.'

See him set to work with zeal
all scripture learnt by heart
that surely the great Lord himself
had set this boy apart.

Alas that old familiar wind
of change found him one day
and with a sigh and
thoughtful brow
he homeward bound
did make his way.

Stepping in the door
he of course began to say
'Why Ma' but wait...
no mother there.
Instead a note lay written:

'George indeed I know it dear,
no need to stay and listen.
I've gone away on holiday
so could you feed the kitten?'

'Night Out'

Boom goes the beat
the clubbers are moving
drinks in their hand
they're casually grooving,

looking around for
someone to raise
the energy level
be in Jesus or devil.

Then he appears
the mystery mover
shuffling his feet
like a juddery hover.

Boom ba doom da
the feet change in time
arms in a looseness
the muscles now primed.

Raise your hands people
let's blow off the roof.
Pump it up louder
stamp your foot like a hoof!

Get into groups
and Egyptianise,
now do Indian belly
with jazz hand surprise!

Security men
look almost, well, scared
shaking their heads
for this not prepared.

'Good Lord, they're all mad.
I've never seen it though
such a herding cafuffle
in any club I've been to'

Now we get a change of beat
a Michael Jackson plucking feet,
so let's slow it down a bit
and pigeon head to each main beat.

Now get into partners please,
guide a twirl and be at ease.
Now roll in and don't feel dumb
at least this move won't
hurt the knees.

Now we return
to the beat from before
for the final song
though all still want more.

Oh joy, it's 'don't stop
believing' people,
oh what a tune,
get high as a steeple!

Now all pile out
with a 'raa blaa' of noise
girls looking sleepy
beware of the boys!

'Man that was fun,
you had a good night?
Let's go back next week
and rock that beat bright.

And shake off the dust
from the lectures we've had
and fill up our spirits
and go a bit mad!'

'ADULTEROUS ADDICTION'

My wife has a weakness for palate,
for sweet things she overly cares.
Sometimes I think she would rather
be married to a chocolate éclair,

or a giant sweet toffee apple
or a silky smooth galaxy bar
or a big bag of popcorn
or a wrapped-chocolate
assortment jar.

Does she know how stupid she looks?
Does her stomach not
say to the brain,
'look here, stop trying to explode me
it's too much, are you insane?'

She cheats on me all day long
lusting for American cookies,
it's honestly plainly absurd
like an addict always at the bookies.

One night I came home from work,
I found her alone by the bed.
She was guilty by this fact
when I turned on the
light she was red.

Red with passion in the form of jam
smeared all over her face
and the filthy clothes of
jam doughnuts disposed
by the door where
they had first embrace.

I could smell the scent of his sugar
lingering gross in the air
and I found him at last
by the involved milk glass,
I warned him 'you'd better beware.'

'I'd finish you off in a second
and sweet my revenge it would taste.
To think a mere doughnut
could take captive my woman,
well villain, your hope is misplaced.

And with that I threw him asunder
into the waste paper bin.
He bled to death there all over
corpses of past lovers therein.

She ran over to me and she cried
'Oh darling please don't be cross.
He tried to force himself on me.
I told him I did to get lost.

But he wore some toxic perfume
that sent me quite into a trance
and I was not myself my love
when I succumbed
to his sumptuous glance.

'There, there my dear, I forgive you
but please, you're breaking my heart.
I can offer much more than
any doughnut or bar
what say you? Let's make a new start.

Fast forward a year and oh bliss
my wife is reformed from her ways,
not a sweetie in sight
and I've searched alright,
no longer the guilt in her gaze.

It's true she's addicted to cheese
and is quite the adulterer with ham
and bread crumbs I find
on the floor by the rind
but not a drop worth of jam!

'BEAUTY AND THE BEAST'

Once upon a time
in a land far away
there lived a lovely princess
and with her lived a prince.

She was very beautiful
with long shiny hair,
he was tall and strong
and for her did really care.

They'd gaze into each other's eyes
his hand upon her cheek
and so firm were his fingers
that her knees would go all weak.

Hand in hand, side by side
they'd walk the dusty road
and stopped at the horizon
to watch the sunset go.

He placed her on a stallion white
and then did take the reins
and rode them 'cross the desert plain
'til stopping to explain.

'You know you're never going back
I've stolen you away.
I've claimed you as my own my dear
the story starts today.'

We came upon a village
in much merriment.
He lead her through the
bustling streets
and to a tavern went.

'Sit down my girl and
wait right there
I'm getting you a drink.'
She missed him already
though he'd been gone a blink.

He happ'ly soon was there again,
two beers firm in hand.
'Drink this up, you'll need it
if with me you want to stand.'

Before she knew it, up she was,
direct to the dance board
where a band of strings began
to strike up the first chord.

The folks looked round all curious
at what then did proceed,
a whirling and a twirling
as this hero took the lead.

He stepped fore-back
and side to side,
and gently held one hand
and then did guide a pirouette
as if it were all planned.

He spun her round and then did lift
her clear off from the ground
and from the marvelling
crowd about
applause did brightly sound.

Then others joined and
wine was poured
and she was blushing so.
He was so amazing,
surely her he mustn't know.

Away in a corner
a cloakèd one did sit,
a comfort to her this dark one
to him she attracted.

But no sooner had she sat
he threw o'er her a sack
and bound her tight and took her off
to some night lair quite black.

He tortured her for days
with whips and sharpened blades
until she had no strength to scream
but 'lone was left to bleed.

Then one day, a day before
her hope and heart would stop
someone did knock down the door
and with some trusted prop

did bravely fight a duel
with this evil interceptor
until he did cut off his head
and come through as the victor.

His presence banished all the dark
like bright light had appeared.
He took her firmly in his arms
and out from what she'd feared.

Suff'ring many tender hours
he bathed her many wounds
whilst she remained unconscious
by evil near consumed.

I didn't give up everything
upon that splintered cross
to lose the one I've chose
over whom I am the boss.

I'll change you if you ask
wash that fear away
until you stand to dance with me
and never shy away.

'But Lord I'll be unfaithful
I'll hurt you.' 'Yes I know'
said he, 'but I'll forgive you
because I love you so.'

'THE BOAT RACE, 2010'

Waves lap against the bank
there's a stillness in the air;
Camera crews unravel leads,
for filming they prepare.

People gather in the club,
a bounteous buffet's spread
radish, salmon, small beef balls...
most leave overfed.

To look along the river bank,
is now to see full length,
spectators ready with their cheers
to give the lads more strength.

Someone's made a funny hat,
a boat upon the top
and photos of the uni teams
in flowers that they've cropped.

The boys file out now one by one
with introduction brief;
The crowd go 'wooo' and
then we watch
which team will know that grief?

They're away from Putney bridge
each stroke exactly matched;
neck and neck they speed on down,
this is Easter race is hatched!

Trailed by scores of boats,
the key one just behind,
check the oars don't get too close
with cheating p'rhaps in mind!

Watching from the boathouse;
some with bated breath;
'Go on there Cambridge,
catch them up
see Oxford to their death.'

One enthusiast I quote,
'it's all about the win'
and yet I think the taking part
means more than just the fin.

But oh what jubilation
just from seeing theirs;
The Cambridge crews have won it
they're rejoicing in their pairs!

About the place a charming buzz
as tearful hugs are made:
Proud parents, friends
and students feel
the force of such a day!

All wash out just like the tide
which having come right in
and soaked somebody's picnic
runs out with the gin!

Now the banks are clearing,
a pair of parakeets display
their love for one another
on this historic day!

'ORIGAMI FRIEND'

Did you fold me with
paper on fine day
while kicking back, relaxing
at the Gods' cafe?
Were there others to help
you as you planned
or did you simply fold
and fold again
to form by chance?
Was it cluttered the table,
did you smoke?
As the paper creatures come to life
do they laugh and joke? 'til I cry...

Hold me again, your
little origami friend.
Refold me again, get out your
glitter glue, your pen.
I need new stickers please,
a sequin here, some shiny leaves.
I need new stickers please,
a shiny gem beside the crease.

Hold me again, your
little origami friend
Refold me again, get out your
glitter glue, your pen.
I'll be a paper plane to fly
across so free again.
I'll be a happy frog to paper
spring across the log.
I'll be a robin red to sing
all day to you instead.

Did you fold me with
paper, one fine day?
As dragons fly with fiery
breath, you fold away.
Did you make her with paper,
the stencilled kind?
As giants climb the moon tall
trees, you fold so fine.
Did you fold me with
paper the secret way,
as fairies flock to watch you
by the window bay?
'til I cry...

Hold me again, your
little origami friend.
Refold me again, get out your
glitter glue, your pen.
I need new stickers please,
a sequin here, some shiny leaves.
I need new stickers please,
a shiny gem beside the crease.

Hold me again your little
origami friend.
Refold me again, get out your
glitter glue, your pen.
I'll be a butterfly, with gems
that sparkle as I fly.
I'll be a peacock proud,
stick more feathers
with the crowd.
I'll be a happy frog to paper
spring across the log.
I'll be a robin red, to sing
all day to you instead.

Did you fold me with paper?

'SPRINGTIME'

Flowers loose their water drops
from petals soft and bright,
glowing in the waiting dark,
still open after light.

Of daffodils I speak really
nodding on the rise.
You find them by the roundabout
taking in the skies,

and in amongst the crocuses
of purple and of blue
of petals curling side on side,
flapping silky smooth.

The grass around is jewels of green
so baby and fluorescent,
growing right before your eyes
making bare earth pleasant.

Birdsong joys and thrills around
as wrens and robin flitter,
strong on their pretty wings
with black pin eyes that glitter.

The water of the broad canal
ripples in the breeze
and breaks with geese, they
plunge their heads
with vigour and with ease.

Further down, the swans they glide,
Mysterious meets Majestic,
shaking out their snow white coats,
Sir Poise and there Miss Prestige.

Little bunnies bob their tails
on dusty ground beneath the trees.
With gentle eyes they peer at you
then into burrows squeeze.

Squirrels scurry up those tree trunks,
bushy tails and steady,
held in curve above their head,
for swiftest motion ready.

Let's brace ourselves for weather,
the skies get their spring clean.
The fluffy clouds are cloths,
the biggest ones you've seen!

River Wey, Guildford

The Weyside

Holy St Trinity

St Nick's

St Saviour's

The Three Pigeons

'The Sea giant' comes from the heart of childhood days by the seaside. The poem anthropomorphises the sea as some living creature, a guardian of all animals within. When you stand in the waves, the regularity of their coming in and going out, their gentle crashing, it feels like breathing. It's such a source of wonder as a child to be on the huge beach, beneath the huge cliffs, beside the huge sea, dwarfed by a system far larger than yourself, at work and alive. I particularly used to love when the tide was out, as it is in the life of this poem.

'The dogs and the guinea pigs' again is true to a childhood experience. Our pet dogs did indeed crush the guinea pig cage and eat the two resident guinea pigs as described in the poem! The leading dog did indeed escape from the garden and get run over as well, as in the poem! The fairy tale comes in the idea that the guinea pigs engineered her fate - their spirits opening back gates and driving vans over undeserving dogs! I wanted to include the happy ending of them all 'reconciled' in heaven. A funny poem, a silly poem, a story my family won't forget!

'Geeky indecision' strikes a chord with a few people I know, regarding switching courses at university. I am fond of the character of the poem, a geeky, lanky, snorting but brilliant teenager, who so longs to change the world and achieve something really worthwhile. In-between each change of study, his eloquence and starry eyed desire is offset by his down to earth mother who offers a listening ear and adds more humour by the contrast. The poem has a bathos end-looking after a kitten after all the hopes of greatness; No matter what heights of fancy study you achieve, it seems it's the simple things in life we come back to- basic home keeping, looking after pets, looking after children. My mum often has asked me to look after the family dog, Lily, when she's away. Caring for something other than yourself seems to me one of the most important things in life!

'Adulterous addiction' is inspired by a binge eating problem I had during my uni days. In the bible, greed is considered a form of idolatry- like you are bowing to a god other than the living one. It's like cheating on God! Hence the poem, which imagines a wife who is cheating on her husband but with food! The illustration to accompany is a little dark- a mars bar man lies in a pool of blood, murdered by the raging husband. It's meant to be funny, (hope no-one is offended on viewing!) and indeed the poem ends happily with the wife character reforming her eating habits as indeed I did. I felt like I was offending the lord with my binge eating and so to reform my ways I'm sure made him happier! God helped me out of it and probably finds it funny in the end as I hope you find this poem!

'Night Out' is a celebration of having a good ol' dance up! The poem is set in a club, reminiscent of the clubs I used to go to in Nottingham. Some people say you shouldn't go clubbing as a Christian but I have to say I don't regret the energy and joy of dancing to the old familiar tracks. Again it's through Christ that I can be a good dancer or at least go for it whatever having been pretty shy before. He is after all lord of the dance and indeed the star mover who gets everyone excited in the poem is a nod to him. The rhythm for the first half is dactylic meter, ie. dum de de dum de de, but then switches to trochaic, ie. dum de dum de dum de, as the new song plays on the overhead, a Michael Jackson number. The switch back to dactylic, dum de de dum de de, matches a change again in song. This keeps up the dynamic nature of the poem.'

'Beauty and the beast' is a simple ballad about two lovers in some far off paradise. However, the lady gets abducted and has to be rescued. The background of the story is again a nod to Jesus. He is better than a lover, and hence the paragon hero in the poem. When the girl attracts to the dark villain, this represents times when I have been attracted to more shadowy ways and have then felt depressed or unhappy or lonely-not quite as extreme as the suffering in the poem about becoming physically scarred; I included this for a greater sense of story. When Jesus rescues, you feel safe and happy and at home again, every time, as the heroine feels in the poem. She is anxious that she will stray to darkness and lose him again. His reply is he will forgive which of course Jesus does whenever we truly seek to change.

'The Boat race' celebrates the Oxford-Cambridge boat race of 2010. My brother was part of the Cambridge boat of rowers that year and the family went to cheer him on. There were several highlights of the experience for me I wanted to convey, one was being surrounded by very posh people, the great nibbles we had at the pavilion, the passion of the watching crowd, and the sight of a pair of green parakeets at the end of the day! In the illustration I wanted to focus on the element of community that such an event brings, folks united in their cheers, a chance for friends to get together, a getting out in the open. So the art features a cheering group of students, the boats themselves merely hinted at by the water in the foreground. Rowing is great, my brother's achievements amazing, but for me that's what I take away-the excitement of the crowd! I hope you get that from the poem and feel a bit warm inside!

'Origami friend' is less a poem and more the lyrics to a self composed song; I enjoy origami as a hobby and had the thought that maybe God planned us with paper folding rather than mud moulding! Dwelling on the illustration more than the lyrics here, the art I hope captures the scene of the song- Gods are considering in a cafe in a time of mythical creatures, each planning a world of their own perhaps- our God featured with the fiery hair, folding his creation with friends at his side. Beyond the window you can see a giant's foot and giant leaves fallen from his hair, caught while climbing the 'moon tall trees'! A distant dragon breathes his best in flames and of course the 'fairies flock to watch by the window bay' as the folding is in swing. On the table are the origami creations in the song, a peacock proud with his feathers, the frog with his paper spring, the butterfly with her gems, the paper plane and the sequined paper ready for humanisation! The idea of course is that we each ourselves were folded from the magic paper. It's an alternative to the creation story, just a bit of fun!

'Spring time' is a heart cry of the season. It is an attempt to capture the realities of spring elements in language that is poetic but also easy to understand. The rhythm is a deliberate alteration between iambic/ trochaic quatrameter and then trimeter in each verse. The rhyme scheme is ABCB as indeed, you may have noticed, for all the poems this time round!

Printed in the United States
By Bookmasters